JUN   2010

For Abby, whose birthday cake inspired this book

Jo Saxton

F

FRANCES LINCOLN
CHILDREN'S BOOKS

Here is a tale about a snail,
an art-loving snail with a silvery trail.

He's small but colourful, clever and sweet.
If you follow his trail you're in for a treat.

There's a special picture I'd like you to see.
A famous artist based it on me!

Turn the pages of my book
and I will teach you how to look.

This picture's tall, but it's too black.
My portrait doesn't look like that.

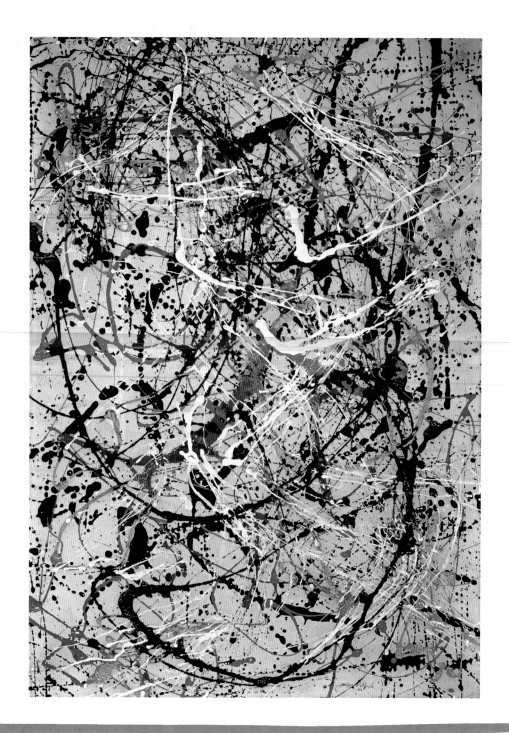

Here there are drips as well as drops.
My picture, though, is built of blocks.

This is better, but do you see? The squares in this picture don't look like me.

This strange painting is far too hot.
Melting clocks and desert rocks?
A place for a snail – this is not!

Well, this one's cooler – but it's too blue! Mine has more orange and lilac too.

Hooray! We've found it!
Can you see?
THIS is Matisse's portrait of
ME!

He's made my body a block of blue,
with my shell a spiral of every hue.

An orange border makes the frame.
This picture brought us both great fame.

It's now in a London gallery –
I hope one day you'll come and see!

When Matisse made my picture he was an old man, recovering from an illness which had weakened him. Young art students often helped him to work at this time. They painted sheets of paper in many different colours for Matisse, and he cut or tore them into the shapes he wanted. The students then hung the pieces on a wall just as he told them to, and when he felt everything looked just right, they were stuck down. This way of making a picture is usually called 'collage' but Matisse liked to call it 'painting with scissors', and you can see him doing that here.

PICTURE CREDITS

Please note: the pages in this book are not numbered. The story begins on page 6.

Page 11: *Abraham*, 1949, Barnett Newman, The Museum of Modern Art, New York.
© ARS, NY and DACS, London 2008. © Photo SCALA, Florence/The Museum of Modern Art,
New York

Page 12: *Number 20*, 1949, Jackson Pollock. © The Pollock-Krasner Foundation ARS,
NY and DACS, London 2008. Private Collection/James Goodman Gallery, New York/
The Bridgeman Art Library

Page 15: *White Center (Yellow, Pink and Lavender on Rose)*, 1950, Mark Rothko, Private Collection.
© 1998 Kate Rothko Prizel & Christopher Rothko ARS, NY and DACS, London.

Page 16: *1940–42 (two forms)*, Ben Nicholson, Southampton City Art Gallery. © Angela Verren
Taunt 2008. All rights reserved, DACS. Photo ©Southampton City Art Gallery, Hampshire/
The Bridgeman Art Library

Pages 18–19: *The Persistence of Memory*, 1931, Salvador Dali, The Museum of Modern Art, New
York. © Salvador Dali, Gala-Salvador Dali Foundation, DACS, London 2008. © Photo SCALA,
Florence/The Museum of Modern Art, New York

Page 21: *Maya in a Sailor Suit*, 1938, Pablo Picasso, The Museum of Modern Art, New York.
© Succession Picasso/DACS. © Photo SCALA, Florence/The Museum of Modern Art,
New York

Page 22: *The Goldfish*, 1912, Henri Matisse, The Pushkin Museum of Fine Art, Moscow.
© Succession H Matisse/DACS 2008

Pages 25 and 27: *The Snail (L'Escargot)*, 1953, Henri Matisse. © Succession H Matisse/
DACS 2008/Tate, London 2008

Page 28: *Photo of Henri Matisse in his workshop*, 1953. Photo by Hélène Adant/RAPHO/
Camera Press, London

SNAIL TRAIL copyright © Frances Lincoln Limited 2009
Text and illustrations copyright © Jo Saxton 2009

First published in Great Britain in 2009 and in the USA in 2010 by
Frances Lincoln Children's Books, 4 Torriano Mews, Torriano Avenue,
London NW5 2RZ

www.franceslincoln.com

British Library Cataloguing in Publication Data available on request

ISBN: 978-1-84780-021-3

Illustrated with collage
Set in TodaySB

Printed in China

9 8 7 6 5 4 3 2 1